IF FOU

Greater Than a Tourist Book Series
Reviews from Readers

I think the series is wonderful and beneficial for tourists to get information before visiting the city.

-Seckin Zumbul, Izmir Turkey

I am a world traveler who has read many trip guides but this one really made a difference for me. I would call it a heartfelt creation of a local guide expert instead of just a guide.

-Susy, Isla Holbox, Mexico

New to the area like me, this is a must have!

 -Joe, Bloomington, USA

This is a good series that gets down to it when looking for things to do at your destination without having to read a novel for just a few ideas.

-Rachel, Monterey, USA

Good information to have to plan my trip to this destination.

-Pennie Farrell, Mexico

Great ideas for a port day.

-Mary Martin USA

Aptly titled, you won't just be a tourist after reading this book. You'll be greater than a tourist!

-Alan Warner, Grand Rapids, USA

Even though I only have three days to spend in San Miguel in an upcoming visit, I will use the author's suggestions to guide some of my time there. An easy read - with chapters named to guide me in directions I want to go.

-Robert Catapano, USA

Great insights from a local perspective! Useful information and a very good value!

-Sarah, USA

This series provides an in-depth experience through the eyes of a local. Reading these series will help you to travel the city in with confidence and it'll make your journey a unique one.

-Andrew Teoh, Ipoh, Malaysia

>TOURIST

GREATER THAN A TOURIST- NORTH CAROLINA USA

50 Travel Tips from a Local

Rachel Beatty

Greater Than a Tourist- North Carolina Copyright © 2018 by CZYK Publishing LLC. All Rights Reserved.

All rights reserved. No part of this book may be reproduced in any form or by any electronic or mechanical means including information storage and retrieval systems, without permission in writing from the author. The only exception is by a reviewer, who may quote short excerpts in a review.

The statements in this book are of the authors and may not be the views of CZYK Publishing or Greater Than a Tourist.

Cover designed by: Ivana Stamenkovic
Cover Image: https://pixabay.com/en/fontana-dam-north-carolina-lake-415847/

Edited by:

CZYK Publishing Since 2011.

Greater Than a Tourist
Visit our website at www.GreaterThanaTourist.com

Lock Haven, PA
All rights reserved.
ISBN: 9781728828008

>TOURIST

>TOURIST

50 TRAVEL TIPS FROM A LOCAL

BOOK DESCRIPTION

Are you excited about planning your next trip?

Do you want to try something new?

Would you like some guidance from a local?

If you answered yes to any of these questions, then this Greater Than a Tourist book is for you.

Greater Than a Tourist- North Carolina USA gives you the inside scoop on the state of North Carolina. Most travel books tell you how to travel like a tourist. Although there is nothing wrong with that, as part of the Greater Than a Tourist series, this book will give you travel tips from someone who has lived at your next travel destination.

In these pages, you will discover advice that will help you throughout your stay. This book will not tell you exact addresses or store hours but instead will give you excitement and knowledge from a local that you may not find in other smaller print travel books.

Travel like a local. Slow down, stay in one place, and get to know the people and the culture. By the time you finish this book, you will be eager and prepared to travel to your next destination.

\>TOURIST

TABLE OF CONTENTS

BOOK DESCRIPTION
TABLE OF CONTENTS
DEDICATION
ABOUT THE AUTHOR
HOW TO USE THIS BOOK
FROM THE PUBLISHER
OUR STORY
WELCOME TO
\> TOURIST
INTRODUCTION
1. The Outer Banks
2. North Carolina Aquariums
3. Museum of the Bizarre
4. Goldsboro Nuclear Mishap
5. Littleton, NC
6. The Country Doctor Museum
7. William Jeffreys' Tomb
8. Marbles Kids Museum and IMAX Theater
9. North Carolina Museum of Art
10. North Carolina Museum of Natural Science
11. Pullen Park
12. Falls Lake
13. Museum of Life and Science
14. Duke Gardens

15. Duke Lemur Center
16. Myers House
17. Creation Museum
18. Devil's Tramping Ground
19. North Carolina Zoo
20. Elsewhere
21. World's Largest Chest of Drawers
22. Körner's Folly
23. Old Salem
24. North Carolina Transportation Museum
25. Mt. Airy
26. Discovery Place
27. Musical Parking Garage
28. Carowinds
29. Tweetsie Railroad
30. Original Mast General Store
31. Grandfather Mountain
32. Linville Falls
33. Craggy Gardens
34. Elijah Mountain Gem Mine
35. Apple Valley Model Railroad Club
36. WNC Nature Center
37. Asheville Pinball Museum
38. Dog City USA
39. Biltmore Estate
40. The Odditorium Bar

>TOURIST

41. Bent Creek Experimental Forest
42. DuPont State Recreational Forest
43. Blue Ridge Parkway and Pisgah Inn
44. Brevard, NC
45. Cradle of Foresty-Pisgah National Forest
46. Grimshawes Historic Post Office
47. The Road to Nowhere
48. Great Smoky Mountain Railroad
49. Tail of the Dragon
50. Monarch Butterfly Trail

TOP REASONS TO BOOK THIS TRIP

50 THINGS TO KNOW ABOUT PACKING LIGHT FOR TRAVEL

Packing and Planning Tips

Travel Questions

Travel Bucket List

NOTES

DEDICATION

To Matthew, my travel partner, who inspires me to explore

To Jack and Ellie, who are the best hiking partners (until they see a squirrel)

ABOUT THE AUTHOR

Rachel Beatty is North Carolina native, raised north of Raleigh from the age of five, who recently moved to the Asheville area. She enjoys exploring her home state and discovering the hidden wonders with her husband and dogs.

>TOURIST

HOW TO USE THIS BOOK

The Greater Than a Tourist book series was written by someone who has lived in an area for over three months. The goal of this book is to help travelers either dream or experience different locations by providing opinions from a local. The author has made suggestions based on their own experiences. Please do your own research before traveling to the area in case the suggested places are unavailable.

Travel Advisories: As a first step in planning any trip abroad, check the Travel Advisories for your intended destination.
https://travel.state.gov/content/travel/en/traveladvisories/traveladvisories.html

\>TOURIST

FROM THE PUBLISHER

Traveling can be one of the most important parts of a person's life. The anticipation and memories that you have are some of the best. As a publisher of the Greater Than a Tourist book series, as well as the popular 50 Things to Know book series, we strive to help you learn about new places, spark your imagination, and inspire you. Wherever you are and whatever you do I wish you safe, fun, and inspiring travel.

Lisa Rusczyk Ed. D.
CZYK Publishing

OUR STORY

Traveling is a passion of the "Greater than a Tourist" series creator. Lisa studied abroad in college, and for their honeymoon Lisa and her husband toured Europe. During her travels to Malta, an older man tried to give her some advice based on his own experience living on the island since he was a young boy. She was not sure if she should talk to the stranger but was interested in his advice. When traveling to some places she was wary to talk to locals because she was afraid that they weren't being genuine. Through her travels, Lisa learned how much locals had to share with tourists. Lisa created the "Greater Than a Tourist" book series to help connect people with locals. A topic that locals are very passionate about sharing.

>TOURIST

```
WELCOME TO
> TOURIST
```

>TOURIST

INTRODUCTION

"Travel far enough, you meet yourself."

—David Mitchell

Mitchell, David. Cloud Atlas. London, Sceptre, 2004.

North Carolina holds endless surprises. From the eastern coast to the western mountains, this beautiful state never ceases to amaze me. As an avid traveler, I keep my eyes open to the random signs and small-town joys that are hidden throughout. To keep this guide organized, I'll move from east to west, letting you travel across the state.

\>TOURIST

1. THE OUTER BANKS

The banks of North Carolina are more than just beautiful, they
are rich in colonial and pirate history. From Nags Head, Blackbeard's treasure cove, to the disappearing colony of Roanoke, the coast has a lot to offer. Aside from Blackbeard's frequent visit, Nags Head is known for Jockey's Ridge State Park, which has the tallest natural sand dunes along the east coast. To the north, Kitty Hawk holds something for everyone: shops, beaches, and the Wright Brothers National Museum, memorializing the first flight.

To the south, Manteo allows visitors to step back into the Elizabethan era at the Roanoke Island Festival Park and the Elizabethan Gardens. Actors portray colonial settlers, giving history and allowing visitors to participate in colonial games and crafting. Further down the coast is Cape Hatteras—a thin strand of islands where visitors can camp along the beach and climb two of the three historic lighthouses.

2. NORTH CAROLINA AQUARIUMS

The North Carolina Aquariums is a system of four locations, each dedicated to a unique aspect of coastal ecosystems in NC. Roanoke Island is home to the Sea Turtle Assistance and Rehabilitation Center, the Graveyard of the Atlantic exhibit, and local coastal life. Pine Knoll Shores follows water from the peaks of Western Carolina to the open Atlantic. Fort Fisher, my personal favorite, journeys down the Cape Fear River through swamps to the reefs. Lastly, Jennette's Pier shows local ocean life based around the pier and discuss ocean fishing practices. When planning your beach trip, check out the aquarium closest to you.

>TOURIST

3. MUSEUM OF THE BIZARRE

The Museum of the Bizarre is the only museum of its kind in the Wilmington area. It claims the crystal skull of knowledge, ghost deer, and numerous oddities guaranteed to make your skin crawl and your mind question the certainties of science. In addition to the creepy, supernatural, and dead men's hair, the museum also boasts two mazes. The first is the laser vault maze. Take on the role of your favorite villain as you attempt to cross through the laser security to pull off the heist of the century. The second is a dizzying mirror maze, so hold your hands out to avoid running face first into yourself. The Museum of the Bizarre is a unique and hair-raising experience.

4. GOLDSBORO NUCLEAR MISHAP

If you're a fan of American history, especially military history, the site of a potentially devastating Air Force blunder may be right up your alley. In 1962, a B-52G carrying two nuclear bombs left Seymour Johnson Air Force Base with a scheduled midair refuel. However, a leak in the right wing caused damage and the plane was recalled to the base. The pilot lost control of the plane, which crashed in a small town called Faro. Neither nuclear bomb detonated; instead the parachute deployed on one, bringing it gently down, and the other plowed into the ground, disintegrating on impact. The Navy attempted to excavate the area, but flooding prevented success. There is now a grove of tree marking the ground filled with plutonium and uranium.

>TOURIST

5. LITTLETON, NC

This little town hosts walking tours and ghost tours through historic downtown, where people have reported paranormal sightings as far back as the revolutionary period. For more serious ghost hunters, there are lessons in using paranormal detecting equipment and guided investigations of reported activity. Littleton is also home to the Cryptozoology and Paranormal Museum. Rather than oddities, this museum is dedicated to creatures and events not explained by traditional science. Phenomena such as Bigfoot, lake and river monsters, and false cryptids such as the Fiji mermaid are main focal points for visitors. The museum staff stays up to date with sightings and record local activity. This is a neat town to stop in and explore.

6. THE COUNTRY DOCTOR MUSEUM

The Country Doctor Museum in Bailey is dedicated to educating its visitors about rural health care. Knowledgeable docents guide the tours, beginning in the Freeman-Brantley building. You walk from the apothecary through the doctor's office, once Dr. Cornelius', and finish this building in his office, where medical tools that resemble tools of torture are on display. The Carriage House pays tribute to American nurses and discusses the importance of available transportation for rural medicine. Finally, in the Farmer Annex, there are a variety of displays as well as the gift shop. This small museum is one of my favorite finds along the NC highways and well worth the visit.

>TOURIST

7. WILLIAM JEFFREYS' TOMB

Located in my small hometown of Youngsville is a bizarre sight. This unique burial ground is deep in the woods off a small back road. William Jeffreys, former NC senator from Franklin County, had a deep-rooted fear that followed him to his grave: the fear of his corpse being devoured by worms. Driven to hallucinations by Typhoid Fever, he told his family to bury him in rock. His father agreed to this final wish, having the tomb carved into a giant boulder on the edge of the property. The remaining family was buried in a cemetery alongside the boulder. It is important to note that this location is on private property and no longer marked by signs due to vandals, and I do not condone trespassing.

8. MARBLES KIDS MUSEUM AND IMAX THEATER

As a kid, Marbles was an exciting and wonderous playground with endless ways to experience the world around me. This amazing museum uses play to educate children about everything. From community living and interaction to physics to finances, Marbles effectively provides interactive, fun exhibits that allow kids to adventure into the real world in comprehensible scenarios. The intended age range for these exhibits is 10 and under, making it an ideal attraction for families with small children. The museum also features an IMAX theater that plays documentary series as well as feature films. The immersive quality of the theater makes you feel as if you are in the movie alongside the characters, going through the journey with them.

>TOURIST

9. NORTH CAROLINA MUSEUM OF ART

NCMA is a must-visit location for tourists in the Raleigh area. The museum is constantly expanding and renovating to display both classic and modern art. There are twelve primary art collections, which are broken down by region and art period. Travelling exhibits are rotated regularly and feature a vast array of subject matter; past exhibits have included fashion, car design, and nature studies. The museum has two primary buildings and a large property with walking trails and large sculpture displays. I recommend wearing comfortable shoes and taking advantage of the walking audible tours.

10. NORTH CAROLINA MUSEUM OF NATURAL SCIENCE

The skeleton of a blue whale hangs from the ceiling and a rotunda of dinosaurs takes your breath away as you enter this museum. The seven-story, adventure-filled Nature Exploration Center walks visitors through the North Carolina wildlife from the mountains to the sea, discussing the various ecosystems, their history, and how they work. The Nature Research Center gives interactive opportunities for visitors to watch scientists at work and to try their hand at unraveling scientific data and interact with million-year-old meteorites. When planning your visit, consider eating before coming to the museum, which is an all-day event.

>TOURIST

11. PULLEN PARK

Pullen Park is the 5th oldest amusement park in the United States and the 16th oldest in the world. The park is adjacent to NC State University's main campus and has recreational activities for all ages and interests. Whether you want to walk along the beautiful duck ponds or play ball, Pullen has playgrounds, fields, and an art center. Reminiscent of the amusement park days Pullen also features a 1911 Gustave A. Dentzel Menagerie Carousel and a C.P. Huntington train ride. This gorgeous park is a great place to spend an afternoon with family or friends.

12. FALLS LAKE

Falls Lake State Recreation Area is comprised of seven access areas around the shoreline of the 12,000-acre reservoir. There are over 300 campsites that include experiences from RV hookups to primitive tent camping. The various access areas include swimming beaches, picnic pavilions, and boat access ramps for both gasoline powered boats and paddle boats. Spend a day on the lake tubing, fishing, or tanning or use the network of trails to explore the pine woods surrounding the lake. Both biking and hiking trails are open, and park officials encourage anyone using the paths to wear bright colors for your safety. Falls Lake is a family friendly fun for everyone.

>TOURIST

13. MUSEUM OF LIFE AND SCIENCE

Walk among dinosaurs and manipulate the weather at the Museum of Life and Science in downtown Durham. This 84-acre, two-story museum features interactive exhibits, exploration of North Carolina wildlife, and an old-time locomotive that runs through the museum grounds. Learning becomes fun as you get involved with the various science exhibits designed to engage your mind and your body. Understand the role of geometry and build contraptions to gain a new appreciate for the natural world. Take advantage of the scheduled activities to better grasp the exhibits and their significance.

14. DUKE GARDENS

In 1935, over 100 flower beds bloomed on Duke University's grounds for the first time. Now, over 75 years later, the gardens are considered a national architectural treasure. When in bloom, few places rival the beauty of the four distinct gardens. Each garden has its own influences, making them unique and truly an artist's paradise. Stroll by the koi pond in the Historic Gardens, explore local carnivorous plants through the Blomquist Garden, and cross the Japanese arch bridge in the Asiatic Arboretum. Take your time and smell the roses in this picturesque place.

>TOURIST

15. DUKE LEMUR CENTER

Outside of the Madagascar, the Duke Lemur Center has the most diverse population of lemurs in the world. The center promotes community-based conservation through education and non-invasive research procedures. The two enclosure types ensure the mental and physical engagement of the lemurs while facilitating the research process. The Duke Lemur Center offers general tours and premium tours, including private party events. When planning your visit, select the tour that best fits your party and your budget. Gain a better understanding of how these adorable mammals can better illuminate the human physique, take an active step in conserving them, and consider adopting a lemur.

16. MYERS HOUSE

Reexperience the house of horror featured in HALLOWEEN, well, a replica. Extreme fan Kenny Caperton designed the house to be as close to the original home from the front and exterior while making it livable. This homage to Michael Myers in Hillsborough hosts various events which are open to the public. However, if there are no events during your North Carolina visit, you can set up a scheduled visit to tour the Myers House. The biggest event is the annual Halloween Bash, during which the Bogeyman himself returns home. If you're a horror fan, this house is not to be missed.

>TOURIST

17. CREATION MUSEUM

As a Bible Belt museum, this establishment promotes a biblical creationist point of view, claiming no evidence exists for evolution. Regardless of your beliefs regarding the earth's beginning, this strange museum is a culmination of Bible verses, taxidermy, and tools. The Creation Museum, Taxidermy Hall of Fame of NC, and Antique Tool Museum hosts a chaotic array of stuffed animals—both taxidermized and toys, old tools, and a declaration of the TV as a tool of the devil. If you're a fan of award-winning taxidermy, antique tools, or just odd collections, this small stop in Southern Pines is well-worth the time.

18. DEVIL'S TRAMPING GROUND

In the hills of Bear Creek is one of the most haunted places in North Carolina. The Devil's Tramping Ground is a perfectly round circle of barren soil, approximately forty feet in diameter. People have attempted sowing seeds and transplanting vegetation, but whatever is planted within the circle dies rapidly. Animals instinctively cower and refuse to approach, but humans, being stubborn, attempt to stay the night, but never succeed. This haunted area has been recognized for its supernatural effect against nature since the early 1600s. If you're ready to watch the Devil dance at night, consider a visit to his tramping grounds.

>TOURIST

19. NORTH CAROLINA ZOO

The NC zoo is the world's largest natural habitat zoo and is home to over 1,600 animals. Located south of Asheville, this immense zoo is an all-day affair. The zoo recommends planning to spend a minimum of three hours in each section of the zoo to best experience all of the exhibits, which are divided into two sections: North America and Africa. The entrances are far apart, so a shuttle runs between the two, making it easy to walk through the zoo without needing to backtrack to the car. I like to start in the North American division to save the elephants for last. Plan ahead with comfortable shoes, water bottles, and plenty of excitement!

20. ELSEWHERE

Originally a used furniture store turned WWII army supply store owned by Joe and Sylvia Gray, this three-story building became a store of all odds-and-ends following Joe Gray's death. Following Sylvia Gray's death, her grandson decided to visit the old store. Astounded by what he found inside, he decided to open up the store to creative minds and allow artists to create a collaborative living museum that reflects the life and mindset of Sylvia Gray. Elsewhere is now a theater, creative laboratory, and so much more where you become a part of the museum itself. When planning a trip to Greensboro, make sure to stop by this exceptional site.

>TOURIST

21. WORLD'S LARGEST CHEST OF DRAWERS

High Point is the "Home Furnishings Capital of the World," and what better way to commemorate this title than the two world's largest chest of drawers. The initial chest was built in 1926 as the "bureau of information" and has been rebuilt twice, including the addition of 6-foot-tall socks dangling from the drawer. The second was build attached to a local furniture store. Next time you're in the furniture capital, take a stop by the largest dressers in the world.

22. KÖRNER'S FOLLY

This architectural wonder is located in Kernersville and open for tours year-round. Körner intended for this house to serve a few purposes—bachelor pad, entertaining space, and most importantly a showroom for the goods of his decoration and furnishing store. The building was constructed with an odd array of materials, including eight different sizes of brick. The house has multiple levels with ranging ceiling sizes, furniture built into the home, and each room has unlimited options in terms of décor. This unique home is a must-see when travelling in that area.

>TOURIST

23. OLD SALEM

This historic district of Winston-Sale is a living museum where well-educated public historians bring the restored village to life. The district aims to educate visitors about and revitalize the settlement during the 18th to 19th centuries. In addition to the historians are skilled tradesmen who interact with visitors while working their trade, which includes blacksmithing, carpentry, and baking. If you have the chance, make sure you stop by the hat shop to try on a few and find your signature look. When you arrive, start in the visitor center to purchase your tickets and gather background information that will help build appreciation for what you are experiencing.

24. NORTH CAROLINA TRANSPORTATION MUSEUM

What once was Southern Railway Company's largest service station for steam engines is now the NC Transportation Museum in Spencer. Pick up your tickets in the visitor center and prepare to explore the development of transportation. The museum features restored steam and diesel engines, antique and classic cars, and an aviation exhibit with an exact replica of the Wright Flyer. The regular train rides are pulled by a diesel engine and lasts approximately 25 minutes. The museum regularly hosts travelling exhibits and other events such as a Day out with Thomas. This awesome museum is large, so remember to wear comfortable shoes and bring water bottles to stay hydrated.

>TOURIST

25. MT. AIRY

Take a stroll through Mayberry in the hometown of the one and only Andy Griffith. Fans of the show are able to stay in his boyhood home, where he resided from adolescence to high school graduation. He attended elementary school at the building now named Andy Griffith Playhouse, which still offers classes in addition to productions and concerts. Directly next door is the Andy Griffith Museum, which houses the largest collection of Andy Griffith memorabilia. Of course, Aunt Bee's home, the Mayberry courthouse, and Floyd's Barber shop each have their place in Mt. Airy. Step back in time and explore the town that inspired the Andy Griffith Show.

26. DISCOVERY PLACE

Discovery Place is an organized collection of museums that are geared toward encouraging an interest and education in STEM (science, technology, engineering, and math) fields. Discovery Place Science houses Charlotte's only indoor rainforest, a laboratory to see the world the way bugs do, and an engaging exploration of the physics of movement. Discovery Place Nature lets visitors walk through a butterfly pavilion, trail through the woods, and meet opossums, snakes, and other critters up close. Get involved with science and gain a better understanding of how the world works while having a blast.

>TOURIST

27. MUSICAL PARKING GARAGE

The parking garage on 7th Street in Charlotte is not like others. This nine-story garage has transparent rectangles connected to giant red fins scaling the walls. Touching the fins cause them to light up and play music. Different songs play on the hour, and a "ghost" in the garage can cause music to begin playing randomly. A riddle is displayed on the side of the building gives the secret to talking to the ghost. If you're in Charlotte, consider parking in this fun garage.

28. CAROWINDS

The great amusement park of the state straddles the state line between North Carolina and South Carolina. Carowinds is a combination amusement park and water park that is constantly updating to improve and intensify their rides. There are rides and attractions for the whole family at every thrill level and a variety of food options. Each October, Carowinds frees the ghosts and lets the monsters run loose in SCarowinds. However, the haunting doesn't start until the evening to make sure the park is still family-friendly during the day. Bring your families for a fun day of thrills!

>TOURIST

29. TWEETSIE RAILROAD

Tweetsie Railroad is a family-oriented attraction that takes you back into the Wild West. There are a few live entertainment options, beginning with the main event: The Wild West Train Adventure. Ride behind the coal-powered steam train and watch out for bandits. Catch a magic show or opt for the amusement park ride that are reminiscent of a state fair. Rides that spin, fly, and cruise are available for all ages. If you're into the cute and fluffy, there is a petting zoo on the property too. Ride through the wild west and hold tight to your purses in bandit country.

30. ORIGINAL MAST GENERAL STORE

Built on land that legends say was bought with a dog, rifle, and sheepskin, the Mast General Store evolved from the Taylor General Store which began in 1883. William Wellington Mast bought half interest in the 1897 before acquiring the store in 1913. The general store provided a link between farmers, crafters, and companies in the area. Today the original Mast General Store in Valle Crucis still operates as a link between local crafters and the community. Walking into the store is a flashback into the early 1900s. Rubber band guns and candy barrels that are pay by the pound fill the downstairs. This step back into history is an amazing stop.

>TOURIST

31. GRANDFATHER MOUNTAIN

Hike to the top of Grandfather Mountain and cross the mile-high swinging bridge and look down into the chasm below. Brave to climb to the end and dangle your legs over the edge. For those that want to experience the bridge, but are not capable of making the trek, there is now an elevator to the top. A network of trails allow visitors to see the beautiful surroundings and the seven natural habitats that show local wildlife in their home. Don't forget to stop by the nature museum which has two dozen exhibits dedicated to Grandfather Mountain's history and surroundings.

32. LINVILLE FALLS

These falls are the most photographed in the Blue Ridge region and for good reason. Hike to five stunning viewing points via the two available trails, one of which is more strenuous. Each viewpoint provides a different angle of the falls and the surrounding cliffs. I prefer Erwins View Overlook, which gives an amazing panoramic shot of the falls and the river. The Linville Gorge trail is more challenging but does provide an overhead look at the basin beneath the falls. The trails are open year-round so take advantage of your preferred temperatures when you can.

\>TOURIST

33. CRAGGY GARDENS

As an avid hiker, a beautiful trail is hard to resist, none more so than the Craggy Gardens Trail. The trailhead is located at the visitor center at milepost 364 of the Blue Ridge parkway. The lush flora and fauna create a fairytale view as the trail winds through thick rhododendron, wildflower patches, and gnarled trees. The hike climbs to an open, grassy summit that offers a stunning view of the Pisgah National Forest and the prominent high peaks of the Blue Ridge Mountains. The trail works its way back to the visitor center past wild blueberry bushes, so don't forget to grab a berry bucket before heading out.

34. ELIJAH MOUNTAIN GEM MINE

Become an 1800s prospector sifting through dirt to find real gemstones and gold that are yours to keep. Ranked the number one gem mine in North Carolina, Elijah Mountain Gem Mine provides everything you need to strike it rich. They have a covered outdoor water flumes and inside flumes to ensure that mining is available every day, rain or shine. Inside they have a koi and goldfish pond as well as adorable baby goats for petting. Their shop is one-of-a-kind too. In addition to the expected fossils and gems are wood carvings, furs, and Native American artifacts. Take time to explore the mountain once you've finished mining and see the beauty surrounding Elijah Mountain.

>TOURIST

35. APPLE VALLEY MODEL RAILROAD CLUB

If you're a fan of the railroad and enjoy model train layouts, this railroad club in Hendersonville is a great stop in a sweet town. Located in the Historic Hendersonville, NC Railroad Depot, the Apple Valley Model Railroad Club has been meeting regularly to construct and run their extensive layouts since 1992. What began as a small replica of the local railroads has expanded into a four room HO scale layout covering much of Western Carolina's operating railroad system. They have a G scale layout outside that runs Climaxes, Shays, and Thomas the Tank Engine. Before you leave, you can't miss Little Pauline, a miniature steam engine build in 1910. She stands 7.5 ft long and 26 inches long. The members of the club are kind and love to answer questions, so stop by the Apple Valley Model Railroad Club.

36. WNC NATURE CENTER

The WNC Nature Center contains forty acres of Appalachian habitat, furthering conservation efforts toward the area's distinct biodiversity. Located just outside of downtown Asheville, the center is convenient for planning an Asheville get away. This amazing conservation and rehabilitation center features our local wildlife, from black bears and cougars to river otters and raccoons. Their goal is to educate visitors about the creatures in their backyard. In addition to conserving the animals, the WNC Nature Center is energy efficient, working to improve our habitat too. Plan around two and a half hours to walk around and experience the entire center.

>TOURIST

37. ASHEVILLE PINBALL MUSEUM

Whether you have children or are a child at heart, the Asheville Pinball Museum is a great place to spend the day. No need to hoard quarters beforehand because once you've paid the admission fee, you have unlimited access to over eighty pinball and classic arcade machines. Like a classic arcade, the museum is dimly lit with machines from wall to wall. However, it has the added benefit of a bar offering snacks, sodas, and beers. The nostalgia is overwhelming for those remembering fun before the Internet invasion, so stop in and get your game on.

38. DOG CITY USA

Asheville is one of the most dog friendly cities in America. Breweries, restaurants, and shops offer bowls of water and customized dishes for our four-legged friends. A great place to start is the first official Dog Welcome Center. Located inside the Dog Door Behavior Center and DogHugger Outfitters, the welcome center has free goodies, doggy commodities, and information about their top 100 dog-friendly locations around town. No matter what you're looking to do with your best furry pal, there are options for you, including places specifically catered toward your dogs. One such place is Woof Gang Bakery and Grooming, which provides high-end products and organic food options. They also offer grooming, day care, and veterinary services. Bring your pups and explore Asheville together.

>TOURIST

39. BILTMORE ESTATE

The Biltmore Estate is one of the biggest attractions of Asheville, and it's not hard to see why. This 250-room castle sits on 8,000 acres dedicated to George Vanderbilt's work in sustainability and environmental protection. The Biltmore Estate is a masterpiece of architecture and gardening that everyone should experience at least once while here. When planning your trip, buy your tickets ahead of time to save money. While the general admission does include self-guided tours of the castle and grounds, I recommend the guided tour to fully understand the estate, its history, and its importance. Prepare for a full day of beauty, no matter what time of year; however, they do offer seasonal events so keep an eye out for what interests you.

40. THE ODDITORIUM BAR

This bar in Asheville is a bizarre blend of art gallery, concert hall, and museum on top of the alcohol service. There are nightly events featuring the best bands in Asheville, burlesque shows, and other entertainers from the area. A macabre, almost uncomfortable, vibe flows through the bar as the décor resembles the dark and fringe. Taxidermy, bones, and artifacts reminiscent of a freak show carnival fill the building, and some of these oddities are for sale. Take home a two-headed duckling or post-mortem photos. This bar is a great way to connect to local artists, get a drunk, and spend an evening out surrounding by the bizarre and unusual.

>TOURIST

41. BENT CREEK EXPERIMENTAL FOREST

As the oldest federal experimental forest east of the Mississippi, Bent Creek was established to research rehabilitation and sustainability. Demonstration areas and research studies provide a hands-on way to understand different forest management styles and their results. Located within the boundaries of Bent Creek are the NC Arboretum and Lake Powhatan recreation area, which has swimming and camping. There are biking, hiking, and horse back riding trails to explore, and each trailhead sign designates the rules of the trail. Come wander through the forest, swim in the lake, and learn about forest management and sustainability.

42. DUPONT STATE RECREATIONAL FOREST

If you're a fan of the Hunger Games, DuPont State Recreational Forest is one site of filming, and there's no surprise why. DuPont is home to 86 miles of trails and several waterfalls. The most common hiking trail is a three-mile trip to three unique waterfalls—Hooker, Triple, and High Falls. The hike is primarily uphill, so wear comfortable shoes, bring water bottles, and be prepared to take breaks as needed. Stop by the visitor center for maps and guidance before heading out into the woods. This trail is dog-friendly, meaning your furry friend can tag along and make new dog friends.

>TOURIST

43. BLUE RIDGE PARKWAY AND PISGAH INN

The Blue Ridge Parkway begins in northern Virginia and winds through the mountains 469 miles, ending in Cherokee, North Carolina. This expansive route provides unending photographic views with various coves and overlooks to pull into and admire the most beautiful part of a gorgeous state. My Sunday nights are spent watching the sunset from the Mills River Valley Overlook as the sky turns vibrant pink and orange. From sunrise to sunset, the mountains are stunning, and on clear nights, the Milky Way is jaw-dropping.

If the drives and views build an appetite, I recommend the Pisgah Inn's restaurant. The chefs prepare daily specials that are mouth-watering and a chocolate cake that makes others pale in comparison. The quality is beyond worth the price, and it is a local favorite on the parkway.

44. BREVARD, NC

Settled along the edge of the Pisgah National Forest, this quaint town forty minutes south of Asheville offers a one-screen movie theater, endless hiking trails, and the annual White Squirrel Festival. The heart of the town lies at the crossing of E. Broad Street and Main Street. Though modernity has reached the town, the downtown shops and restaurants demonstrate the rich history of Brevard. Across from the White Squirrel Shoppe sits O.P. Taylor's, which houses two stories of toys, both modern and old-fashioned. Three stores over is Rocky's Grill and Soda Shop, which serves burgers, hot dogs, and a diverse shake menu. If hotels are not for you, Brevard hosts a variety of AirBnBs and camping options.

>TOURIST

45. CRADLE OF FORESTY– PISGAH NATIONAL FOREST

This American heritage site marks the beginning of science-based forest management and conservation in the United States. Inside the Forest Discovery Center, visitors can interact with the hands-on exhibits, watch a short film about the Biltmore Forest School, and fly over the forest in a helicopter simulator. The trails behind the center are 13 miles long; one branch walks by a 1914 Climax locomotive with logging cars, and the other walks through the original Biltmore campus for forestry. It's a fun walk through the lush forest and make sure to stop in the visitor's center to talk to the friendly volunteers and walk through the gift shop.

46. GRIMSHAWES HISTORIC POST OFFICE

This minute post office was the "Smallest U.S. Post Office" while in operation from 1903-1953. The adorable structure is still intact and standing, located conveniently off Whiteside Cove Road outside of Cashiers. Each of the postmasters of this office were named Grimshawe, hence the name. There are other attractions in Cashiers and Highlands, such as the sliding rock and the Bob Padgett Poplar, which is one of the biggest in the U.S. This little stop is a photographic opportunity that should not be missed.

47. THE ROAD TO NOWHERE

Follow this scenic highway six miles into the Great Smoky Mountains where it ends abruptly at the mouth of a tunnel. Upon building Fontana Lake outside of Bryson City, the government promised to replace Highway 288 and restore access to the communities separated by the lake. However, due to environmental issues, the project was abandoned at the mouth of a tunnel. This beautiful drive passes Fontana Lake and gives access to numerous hiking trails on the other side of the tunnel.

>TOURIST

48. GREAT SMOKY MOUNTAIN RAILROAD

This scenic railroad takes you from the historic depot in Bryson City across the Western Carolina hills. GSMR offers rides behind both diesel and steam engines through various excursions, including the Carolina Moonshine Experience. The coaches are comfortable and are divided by class, which determines the price. This ride is fun for the whole family and full of stunning views. When the train returns, take your time through the Smoky Mountain Trains Museum located in the Bryson City Station. The museum holds over 7,000 Lionel engines, cars, and accessories and runs an impressive layout. Take a day ride with the Great Smoky Mountain Railroad and see Western Carolina from a new point of view.

49. TAIL OF THE DRAGON

The Tail of the Dragon, aka US-129, is a mountain pass highway that rolls along the North Carolina and Tennessee border. This eleven-mile stretch of road holds 318 curves. Rather than sight-seeing, the road itself is the attraction for thrill seekers and speed enthusiasts. If you think it looks like a scene from an adventure film, check out the photos of your car online after the drive. There are two sponsored photographers that take pictures of your car as you race by. The tight turns and pure adrenaline are exhilarating, worthy of a spot on the bucket it.

50. MONARCH BUTTERFLY TRAIL

Each fall the monarch butterfly travels over 2,000 miles, passing through the western mountains of North Carolina. Travel the Blue Ridge Parkway in late September to early October to prime cove overlooks and watch millions of butterflies fly south for the winter. Naturally, institutions such as the North Carolina Arboretum and the Cradle of Forestry host events to encourage conservation of the monarch butterfly. This gorgeous sight should not be missed.

\>TOURIST

TOP REASONS TO BOOK THIS TRIP

1. Few states can boast the biodiversity and unique history of North Carolina. From the mountains to the sea, this state holds the most beautiful views, bizarre museums, and rich culture.

2. No matter where in the state you go, the paranormal follows. From Biltmore to the Devil's Tramping Grounds to Littleton, the spooky and unexplained is out there for thrill seekers.

3. NC is the birthplace of many favorite franchises, including Bojangles, Red Oak Brewery, and Cheerwine. This home to innovation and development is home to unique flavors and industries that helped create the modern America.

BONUS BOOK

50 THINGS TO KNOW ABOUT PACKING LIGHT FOR TRAVEL

PACK THE RIGHT WAY EVERY TIME

AUTHOR: MANIDIPA BHATTACHARYYA

First Published in 2015 by Dr. Lisa Rusczyk. Copyright 2015. All Rights Reserved. No part of this publication may be reproduced, including scanning and photocopying, or distributed in any form or by any means, electronic or mechanical, or stored in a database or retrieval system without prior written permission from the publisher.

Disclaimer: The publisher has put forth an effort in preparing and arranging this book. The information provided herein by the author is provided "as is". Use this information at your own risk. The publisher is not a licensed doctor. Consult your doctor before engaging in any medical activities. The publisher and author disclaim any liabilities for any loss of profit or commercial or personal damages resulting from the information contained in this book.

Edited by Melanie Howthorne

ABOUT THE AUTHOR

Manidipa Bhattacharyya is a creative writer and editor, with an education in English literature and Linguistics. After working in the IT industry for seven long years she decided to call it quits and follow her heart instead. Manidipa has been ghost writing, editing, proof reading and doing secondary research services for many story tellers and article writers for about three years. She stays in Kolkata, India with her husband and a busy two year old. In her own time Manidipa enjoys travelling, photography and writing flash fiction.

Manidipa believes in travelling light and never carries anything that she couldn't haul herself on a trip. However, travelling with her child changed the scenario. She seemed to carry the entire world with her for the baby on the first two trips. But good sense prevailed and she is again working her way to becoming a light traveler, this time with a kid.

INTRODUCTION

He who would travel happily must travel light.

-Antoine de Saint-Exupéry

Travel takes you to different places from seas and mountains to deserts and much more. In your travels you get to interact with different people and their cultures. You will, however, enjoy the sights and interact positively with these new people even more, if you are travelling light.

When you travel light your mind can be free from worry about your belongings. You do not have to spend precious vacation time waiting for your luggage to arrive after a long flight. There is be no chance of your bags going missing and the best part is that you need not pay a fee for checked baggage.

People who have mastered this art of packing light will root for you to take only one carry-on, wherever you go. However, many people can find it really hard to pack light. More so if you are travelling with children. Differentiating between "must have" and "just in case" items is the starting point. There will be ample shopping avenues at your destination which are just waiting to be explored.

This book will show you 'packing' in a new 'light' – pun intended – and help you to embrace light packing practices for all of your future travels.

Off to packing!

DEDICATION

I dedicate this book to all the travel buffs that I know, who have given me great insights into the contents of their backpacks.

THE RIGHT TRAVEL GEAR

1. CHOOSE YOUR TRAVEL GEAR CAREFULLY

While selecting your travel gear, pick items that are light weight, durable and most importantly, easy to carry. There are cases with wheels so you can drag them along – these are usually on the heavy side because of the trolley. Alternatively a backpack that you can carry comfortably on your back, or even a duffel bag that you can carry easily by hand or sling across your body are also great options. Whatever you choose, one thing to keep in mind is that the luggage itself should not weigh a ton, this will give you the flexibility to bring along one extra pair of shoes if you so desire.

2. CARRY THE MINIMUM NUMBER OF BAGS

Selecting light weight luggage is not everything. You need to restrict the number of bags you carry as well. One carry-on size bag is ideal for light travel. Most carriers allow one cabin baggage plus one purse, handbag or camera bag as long as it slides under the seat in front. So technically, you can carry two items of luggage without checking them in.

3. PACK ONE EXTRA BAG

Always pack one extra empty bag along with your essential items. This could be a very light weight duffel bag or even a sturdy tote bag which takes up minimal space. In the event that you end up buying a lot of souvenirs, you already have a handy bag to stuff all that into and do not have to spend time hunting for an appropriate bag.

> *I'm very strict with my packing and have everything in its right place. I never change a rule. I hardly use anything in the hotel room. I wheel my own wardrobe in and that's it.*
>
> Charlie Watts

CLOTHES & ACCESSORIES

4. PLAN AHEAD

Figure out in advance what you plan to do on your trip. That will help you to pick that one dress you need for the occasion. If you are going to attend a wedding then you have to carry formal wear. If not, you can ditch the gown for something lighter that will be comfortable during long walks or on the beach.

5. WEAR THAT JACKET

Remember that wearing items will not add extra luggage for your air travel. So wear that bulky jacket that you plan to carry for your trip. This saves space and can also help keep you warm during the chilly flight.

6. MIX AND MATCH

Carry clothes that can be interchangeably used to reinvent your look. Find one top that goes well with a couple of pairs of pants or skirts. Use tops, shirts and jackets wisely along with other accessories like a scarf or a stole to create a new look.

>TOURIST

7. CHOOSE YOUR FABRIC WISELY

Stuffing clothes in cramped bags definitely takes its toll which results in wrinkles. It is best to carry wrinkle free, synthetic clothes or merino tops. This will eliminate the need for that small iron you usually bring along.

8. DITCH CLOTHES PACK UNDERWEAR

Pack more underwear and socks. These are the things that will give you a fresh feel even if you do not get a chance to wear fresh clothes. Moreover these are easy to wash and can be dried inside the hotel room itself.

9. CHOOSE DARK OVER LIGHT

While picking your clothes choose dark coloured ones. They are easy to colour coordinate and can last longer before needing a wash. Accidental food spills and dirt from the road are less visible on darker clothes.

10. WEAR YOUR JEANS

Take only one pair of Jeans with you, which you should wear on the flight. Remember to pick a pair that can be worn for sightseeing trips and is equally eloquent for dinner. You can add variety by adding light weight cargoes and chinos.

11. CARRY SMART ACCESSORIES

The right accessory can give you a fresh look even with the same old dress. An intelligent neck-piece, a couple of bright scarves, stoles or a sarong can be used in a number of ways to add variety to your clothing. These light weight beauties can double up as a nursing cover, a light blanket, beach wear, a modesty cover for visiting places of worship, and also makes for an enthralling game of peek-a-boo.

12. LEARN TO FOLD YOUR GARMENTS

Seasoned travellers all swear by rolling their clothes for compact and wrinkle free packing. Bundle packing, where you roll the clothes around a central object as if tying it up, is also a popular method of compact and wrinkle free packing. Stacking folded clothes one on top of another is a big no-no as it makes creases extreme and they are difficult to get rid of without ironing.

13. WASH YOUR DIRTY LAUNDRY

One of the ways to avoid carrying loads of clothes is to wash the clothes you carry. At some places you might get to use the laundry services or a Laundromat but if you are in a pinch, best solution is to wash them yourself. If that is the plan then carrying quick drying clothes is highly recommended, which most often also happen to be the wrinkle free variety.

14. LEAVE THOSE TOWELS BEHIND

Regular towels take up a lot of space, are heavy and take ages to dry out. If you are staying at hotels they will provide you with towels anyway. If you are travelling to a remote place, where the availability of towels look doubtful, carry a light weight travel towel of viscose material to do the job.

15. USE A COMPRESSION BAG

Compression bags are getting lots of recommendation now days from regular travellers. These are useful for saving space in your luggage when you have to pack bulky dresses. While packing for the return trip, get help from the hotel staff to arrange a vacuum cleaner.

FOOTWEAR

16. PUT ON YOUR HIKING BOOTS

If you have plans to go hiking or trekking during your trip, you will need those bulky hiking boots. The best way to carry them is to wear them on flight to save space and luggage weight. You can remove the boots once inside and be comfortable in your socks.

17. PICKING THE RIGHT SHOES

Shoes are often the bulkiest items, along with being the dainty if you are a female. They need care and take up a lot of space in your luggage. It is advisable therefore to pick shoes very carefully. If you plan to do a lot of walking and site seeing, then wearing a pair of comfortable walking shoes are a must. For more formal occasions you can carry durable, light weight flats which will not take up much space.

18. STUFF SHOES

If you happen to pack a pair of shoes, ensure you utilize their hollow insides. Tuck small items like rolled up socks or belts to save space. They will also be easy to find.

>TOURIST

TOILETRIES

19. STASHING TOILETRIES

Carry only absolute necessities. Airline rules dictate that for one carry-on bag, liquids and gels must be in 3.4 ounce (100ml) bottles or less, and must be packed in a one quart zip-lock bag. If you are planning to stay in a hotel, the basic things will be provided for you. It's best is to buy the rest from the local market at your destination.

20. TAKE ALONG TAMPONS

Tampons are a hard to find item in a lot of countries. Figure out how many you need and pack accordingly. For longer stays you can buy them online and have them delivered to where you are staying.

21. GET PAMPERED BEFORE YOU TRAVEL

Some avid travellers suggest getting a pedicure and manicure just the day before travelling. This not only gives you a well kept look, you also save the trouble of packing nail polish. Remember, every little bit of weight reduced adds up.

ELECTRONICS

22. LUGGING ALONG ELECTRONICS

Electronics have a large role to play in our lives today. Most of us cannot imagine our lives away from our phones, laptops or tablets. However while travelling, one must consider the amount of weight these electronics add to our luggage. Thankfully smart phones come along with all the essentials tools like a camera, email access, picture editing tools and more. They are smart to the point of eliminating the need to carry multiple gadgets. Choose a smart phone that suits all your requirements and travel with the world in your palms or pocket.

23. REDUCE THE NUMBER OF CHARGERS

If you do travel with multiple electronic devices, you will have to bear the additional burden of carrying all their chargers too. Check if a single charger can be used for multiple devices. You might also consider investing in a pocket charger. These small devices support multiple devices while keeping you charged on the go.

>TOURIST

24. TRAVEL FRIENDLY APPS

Along with smart phones come numerous apps, which are immensely helpful in our travels. You name it and you have an app for it at hand – take pictures, sharing with friends and family, torch to light dark roads, maps, checking flight/train times, find hotels and many other things. Use these smart alternatives to traditional items like books to eliminate weight and save space.

*I get ideas about what's essential
when packing my suitcase.*

-Diane von Furstenberg

TRAVELLING WITH KIDS

25. BRING ALONG THE STROLLER

Kids might enjoy walking for a while but they soon tire out and a stroller is the just the right thing for them to rest in while you continue your tour. Strollers also double duty as a luggage carrier and shopping bag holder. Remember to pick a light weight, easy to handle brand of stroller. Better yet, find out in advance if you can rent a stroller at your destination.

26. BRING ONLY ENOUGH DIAPERS FOR YOUR TRIP

Diapers take up a lot of space and add to the weight of your luggage. Therefore it is advisable to carry just enough diapers to last through the trip and a few for afterwards, till you buy fresh stock at your destination. Unless of course you are travelling to a really remote area, in which case you have no choice but to carry the load. Otherwise diapers are something you will find pretty easily.

27. TAKE ONLY A COUPLE OF TOYS

Children are easily attracted by new things in their environment. While travelling they will find numerous 'new' objects to scrutinize and play with. Packing just one favorite toy is enough, or if there is no favorite toy leave out all of them in favor of stories or imaginary games.

28. CARRY KID FRIENDLY SNACKS

Create a small snack counter in your bag to store away quick bites for those sudden hunger pangs. Depending on the child's age this could include chocolates, raisins, dry fruits, granola bars or biscuits. Also keep a bottle of water handy for your little one.

>TOURIST

These things do not add much weight and can be adjusted in a handbag or knapsack.

29. GAMES TO CARRY

Create some travel specific, imaginary games if you have slightly grown up children, like spot the attractions. Keep a coloring book and colors handy for in-flight or hotel time. Apps on your smart phone can keep the children engaged with cartoons and story books. Older children are often entertained by games available on phones or tablets. This cuts the weight of luggage down while keeping the kids entertained.

30. LET THE KIDS CARRY THEIR LOAD

A good thing is to start early sharing of responsibilities. Let your child pick a bag of his or her choice and pack it themselves. Keep tabs on what they are stuffing in their bags by asking if they will be using that item on the trip. It could start out being just an entertainment bag initially but with growing years they will learn to sort the useful from the superfluous. Children as little as four can maneuver a small trolley suitcase like a pro- their experience in pull along toys credit. If you are worried that you may be pulling it for them, you may want to start with a backpack.

31. DECIDE ON LOCATION FOR CHILDREN TO SLEEP

While on a trip you might not always get a crib at your destination, and carrying one will make life all the more difficult. Instead call ahead to see if there are any cribs or roll out beds for children. You may even put blankets on the floor. Weave them a story about camping and they will gladly sleep without any trouble.

32. GET BABY PRODUCTS DELIVERED AT YOUR DESTINATION

If you are absolutely paranoid about not getting your favourite variety of diaper or brand of baby food, check out online stores like amazon.com for services in your destination city. You can buy things online ahead of your travel and get them delivered to your hotel upon arrival.

33. FEEDING NEEDS OF YOUR INFANTS

If you are travelling with a breastfed infant, you save the trouble of carrying bottles and bottle sanitization kits. For special food, or medications, you may need to call ahead to make sure you have a refrigerator where you are staying.

34. FEEDING NEEDS OF YOUR TODDLER

With the progression from infancy to toddler, their dietary requirements too evolve. You will have to pack some snacks for travelling time. Fresh fruits and vegetables can be purchased at your destination. Most of the cities you travel to in whichever part of the world, will have baby food products and formulas, available at the local drug-store or the supermarket.

35. PICKING CLOTHES FOR YOUR BABY

Contrary to popular belief, babies can do without many changes of clothes. At the most pack 2 outfits per day. Pack mix and match type clothes for your little one as well. Pick things which are comfortable to wear and quick to dry.

36. SELECTING SHOES FOR YOUR BABY

Like outfits, kids can make do with two pairs of comfortable shoes. If you can get some water resistant shoes it will be best. To expedite drying wet shoes, you can stuff newspaper in them then wrap them with newspaper and leave them to dry overnight.

37. KEEP ONE CHANGE OF CLOTHES HANDY

Travelling with kids can be tricky. Keep a change of clothes for the kids and mum handy in your purse or tote bag. This takes a bit of space in your hand luggage but comes extremely handy in case there are any accidents or spills.

38. LEAVE BEHIND BABY ACCESSORIES

Baby accessories like their bed, bath tub, car seat, crib etc. should be left at home. Many hotels provide a crib on request, while car seats can be borrowed from friends or rented. Babies can be given a bath in the hotel sink or even in the adult bath tub with a little bit of water. If you bring a few bath toys, they can be used in the bath, pool, and out of water. They can also be sanitized easily in the sink.

39. CARRY A SMALL LOAD OF PLASTIC BAGS

With children around there are chances of a number of soiled clothes and diapers. These plastic bags help to sort the dirt from the clean inside your big bag.

These are very light weight and come in handy to other carry stuff as well at times.

PACK WITH A PURPOSE

40. PACKING FOR BUSINESS TRIPS

One neutral-colored suit should suffice. It can be paired with different shirts, ties and accessories for different occasions. One pair of black suit pants could be worn with a matching jacket for the office or with a snazzy top for dinner.

41. PACKING FOR A CRUISE

Most cruises have formal dinners, and that formal dress usually takes up a lot of space. However you might find a tuxedo to rent. For women, a short black dress with multiple accessory options will do the trick.

42. PACKING FOR A LONG TRIP OVER DIFFERENT CLIMATES

The secret packing mantra for travel over multiple climates is layering. Layering traps air around your body creating insulation against the cold. The same light t-shirt that is comfortable in a warmer climate can be the innermost layer in a colder climate.

REDUCE SOME MORE WEIGHT

43. LEAVE PRECIOUS THINGS AT HOME

Things that you would hate to lose or get damaged leave them at home. Precious jewelry, expensive gadgets or dresses, could be anything. You will not require these on your trip. Leave them at home and spare the load on your mind.

44. SEND SOUVENIRS BY MAIL

If you have spent all your money on purchasing souvenirs, carrying them back in the same bag that you brought along would be difficult. Either pack everything in another bag and check it in the airport or get everything shipped to your home. Use an international carrier for a secure transit, but this could be more expensive than the checking fees at the airport.

45. AVOID CARRYING BOOKS

Books equal to weight. There are many reading apps which you can download on your smart phone or tab.

Plus there are gadgets like Kindle and Nook that are thinner and lighter alternatives to your regular book.

CHECK, GET, SET, CHECK AGAIN

46. STRATEGIZE BEFORE PACKING

Create a travel list and prepare all that you think you need to carry along. Keep everything on your bed or floor before packing and then think through once again – do I really need that? Any item that meets this question can be avoided. Remove whatever you don't really need and pack the rest.

47. TEST YOUR LUGGAGE

Once you have fully packed for the trip take a test trip with your luggage. Take your bags and go to town for window shopping for an hour. If you enjoy your hour long trip it is good to go, if not, go home and reduce the load some more. Repeat this test till you hit the right weight.

48. ADD A ROLL OF DUCT TAPE

You might wonder why, when this book has been talking about reducing stuff, we're suddenly asking you to pack something totally unusual. This is because when you have limited supplies, duct tape is immensely helpful for small repairs – a broken bag, leaking zip-lock bag, broken sunglasses, you name it and duct tape can fix it, temporarily.

49. LIST OF ESSENTIAL ITEMS

Even though the emphasis is on packing light, there are things which have to be carried for any trip. Here is our list of essentials:

- Passport/Visa or any other ID

- Any other paper work that might be required on a trip like permits, hotel reservation confirmations etc.

- Medicines – all your prescription medicines and emergency kit, especially if you are travelling with children

- Medical or vaccination records

- Money in foreign currency if travelling to a different country

- Tickets- Email or Message them to your phone

>TOURIST

50. MAKE THE MOST OF YOUR TRIP

Wherever you are going, whatever you hope to do we encourage you to embrace it whole-heartedly. Take in the scenery, the culture and above all, enjoy your time away from home.

On a long journey even a straw weighs heavy.

-Spanish Proverb

\>TOURIST

PACKING AND PLANNING TIPS

A Week before Leaving

- Arrange for someone to take care of pets and water plants.
- Stop mail and newspaper.
- Notify Credit Card companies where you are going.
- Change your thermostat settings.
- Car inspected, oil is changed, and tires have the correct pressure.
- Passports and photo identification is up to date.
- Pay bills.
- Copy important items and download travel Apps.
- Start collecting small bills for tips.

Right Before Leaving

- Clean out refrigerator.
- Empty garbage cans.
- Lock windows.
- Make sure you have the proper identification with you.
- Bring cash for tips.
- Remember travel documents.
- Lock door behind you.
- Remember wallet.
- Unplug items in house and pack chargers.

>TOURIST

READ OTHER GREATER THAN A TOURIST BOOKS

Greater Than a Tourist San Miguel de Allende Guanajuato Mexico: 50 Travel Tips from a Local by Tom Peterson

Greater Than a Tourist – Lake George Area New York USA: 50 Travel Tips from a Local by Janine Hirschklau

Greater Than a Tourist – Monterey California United States: 50 Travel Tips from a Local by Katie Begley

Greater Than a Tourist – Chanai Crete Greece: 50 Travel Tips from a Local by Dimitra Papagrigoraki

Greater Than a Tourist – The Garden Route Western Cape Province South Africa: 50 Travel Tips from a Local by Li-Anne McGregor van Aardt

Greater Than a Tourist – Sevilla Andalusia Spain: 50 Travel Tips from a Local by Gabi Gazon

Greater Than a Tourist – Kota Bharu Kelantan Malaysia: 50 Travel Tips from a Local by Aditi Shukla

Children's Book: Charlie the Cavalier Travels the World by Lisa Rusczyk

>TOURIST

> TOURIST

Visit Greater Than a Tourist for Free Travel Tips
http://GreaterThanATourist.com

Sign up for the Greater Than a Tourist Newsletter for discount days, new books, and travel information:
http://eepurl.com/cxspyf

Follow us on Facebook for tips, images, and ideas:
https://www.facebook.com/GreaterThanATourist

Follow us on Pinterest for travel tips and ideas:
http://pinterest.com/GreaterThanATourist

Follow us on Instagram for beautiful travel images:
http://Instagram.com/GreaterThanATourist

>TOURIST

> TOURIST

Please leave your honest review of this book on Amazon and Goodreads. Please send your feedback to GreaterThanaTourist@gmail.com as we continue to improve the series. We appreciate your positive and constructive feedback. Thank you.

>TOURIST

METRIC CONVERSIONS

TEMPERATURE

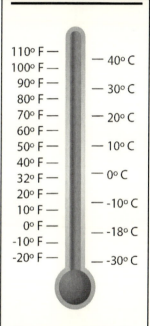

110° F — — 40° C
100° F —
90° F — — 30° C
80° F —
70° F — — 20° C
60° F —
50° F — — 10° C
40° F —
32° F — — 0° C
20° F —
10° F — — -10° C
0° F —
-10° F — — -18° C
-20° F — — -30° C

To convert F to C:

Subtract 32, and then multiply by 5/9 or .5555.

To Convert C to F:
Multiply by 1.8 and then add 32.

32F = 0C

LIQUID VOLUME

To Convert:	Multiply by
U.S. Gallons to Liters	3.8
U.S. Liters to Gallons	.26
Imperial Gallons to U.S. Gallons	1.2
Imperial Gallons to Liters	4.55
Liters to Imperial Gallons	.22

1 Liter = .26 U.S. Gallon
1 U.S. Gallon = 3.8 Liters

DISTANCE

To convert	Multiply by
Inches to Centimeters	2.54
Centimeters to Inches	.39
Feet to Meters	.3
Meters to Feet	3.28
Yards to Meters	.91
Meters to Yards	1.09
Miles to Kilometers	1.61
Kilometers to Miles	.62

1 Mile = 1.6 km
1 km = .62 Miles

WEIGHT

1 Ounce = .28 Grams
1 Pound = .4555 Kilograms
1 Gram = .04 Ounce
1 Kilogram = 2.2 Pounds

>TOURIST

TRAVEL QUESTIONS

- Do you bring presents home to family or friends after a vacation?
- Do you get motion sick?
- Do you have a favorite billboard?
- Do you know what to do if there is a flat tire?
- Do you like a sun roof open?
- Do you like to eat in the car?
- Do you like to wear sun glasses in the car?
- Do you like toppings on your ice cream?
- Do you use public bathrooms?
- Did you bring your cell phone and does it have power?
- Do you have a form of identification with you?
- Have you ever been pulled over by a cop?
- Have you ever given money to a stranger on a road trip?
- Have you ever taken a road trip with animals?
- Have you ever went on a vacation alone?
- Have you ever run out of gas?

- If you could move to any place in the world, where would it be?

- If you could travel anywhere in the world, where would you travel?

- If you could travel in any vehicle, which one would it be?

- If you had three things to wish for from a magic genie, what would they be?

- If you have a driver's license, how many times did it take you to pass the test?

- What are you the most afraid of on vacation?

- What do you want to get away from the most when you are on vacation?

- What foods smells bad to you?

- What item do you bring on ever trip with you away from home?

- What makes you sleepy?

- What song would you love to hear on the radio when you're cruising on the highway?

- What travel job would you want the least?

- What will you miss most while you are away from home?

- What is something you always wanted to try?

\>TOURIST

- What is the best road side attraction that you ever saw?
- What is the farthest distance you ever biked?
- What is the farthest distance you ever walked?
- What is the weirdest thing you needed to buy while on vacation?
- What is your favorite candy?
- What is your favorite color car?
- What is your favorite family vacation?
- What is your favorite food?
- What is your favorite gas station drink or food?
- What is your favorite license plate design?
- What is your favorite restaurant?
- What is your favorite smell?
- What is your favorite song?
- What is your favorite sound that nature makes?
- What is your favorite thing to bring home from a vacation?
- What is your favorite vacation with friends?
- What is your favorite way to relax?

- Where is the farthest place you ever traveled in a car?
- Where is the farthest place you ever went North, South, East and West?
- Where is your favorite place in the world?
- Who is your favorite singer?
- Who taught you how to drive?
- Who will you miss the most while you are away?
- Who if the first person you will contact when you get to your destination?
- Who brought you on your first vacation?
- Who likes to travel the most in your life?
- Would you rather be hot or cold?
- Would you rather drive above, below, or at the speed limited?
- Would you rather drive on a highway or a back road?
- Would you rather go on a train or a boat?
- Would you rather go to the beach or the woods?

>TOURIST

TRAVEL BUCKET LIST

1.

2.

3.

4.

5.

6.

7.

8.

9.

10.

>TOURIST

NOTES

Made in United States
North Haven, CT
15 February 2022

16132933R00071